VILLAGES

OF HISPANIC NEW MEXICO

VILLAGES
OF HISPANIC NEW MEXICO

Text and Photographs by
NANCY HUNTER WARREN

SCHOOL OF AMERICAN RESEARCH PRESS   SANTA FE, NEW MEXICO

SCHOOL OF AMERICAN RESEARCH PRESS
Post Office Box 2188, Santa Fe, New Mexico 87504-2188

Editor: Tom Ireland
Designer: Deborah Flynn Post
Typographer: Casa Sin Nombre
Printer: Dai Nippon

Library of Congress Cataloging-in-Publication Data:

Warren, Nancy Hunter.
    Villages of Hispanic New Mexico.

    Bibliography: p.
    1. Hispanic Americans—New Mexico—Social life and customs. 2. Villages—
New Mexico—Pictorial works. 3. New Mexico—Social life and customs. 4. New
Mexico—Description and travel—1981–   —Views.
F805.S75W37   1987   978.9'00468073   87–12715
ISBN 0-933452-19-5
ISBN 0-933452-20-9 (pbk.)

Cover: Calvario at Gallina Plaza, New Mexico.
Frontispiece: Penitente brother in cap worn during Holy Week. The bulto of
    Nuestro Padre Jesús was made by José Benito Ortega during the late 1800s.

TO BOBBY

whose love of the landscape

led to this village odyssey

CONTENTS

ILLUSTRATIONS

PREFACE

The Hispanic villages of New Mexico became part of my life in 1973, when I began weekly explorations into the rural areas of the state. Driving off the main highways, sometimes along narrow dirt roads, I wandered into many small villages—the survivors of settlements founded by Spanish and Mexican colonists, some as early as the seventeenth century. I discovered old adobe houses with soft lines and simple shapes, often clustered around a church-dominated plaza, cows ambling along a village road, and on a distant hill, a cross silhouetted against the sky. The people introduced me to their fiestas, ancient dance-dramas, and customs that lingered from an earlier way of life.

For twelve years I made frequent visits to the villages, photographing and meeting the people. In the beginning, my motives for being there were sometimes looked upon with suspicion. Many thought it strange that I found beauty in an old building or a time-worn face. The things that I considered important enough to capture on film were thought by the villagers to be ordinary, everyday events—not particularly worth recording. Nevertheless, after many visits and the sharing of photographs, I was gradually accepted as a friend. The villagers fed me dinner and invited me back for the next fiesta or a blessing of the ditch.

These years have been particularly rewarding for me, and I treasure the many friends I have made as well as the chance to experience a different lifestyle. I thank the village people for their kindness and for their indulgence in my ever-present camera. Without their generosity, this glimpse into the Hispanic villages of New Mexico would not have been possible.

My special thanks go to Myra Ellen Jenkins, former New Mexico state historian, for the hours she spent reading the text of this book and correcting my inaccuracies. Her knowledge of New Mexico history helps assure an authenticity I could not have achieved otherwise. David Snow and Orlando Romero also offered advice and assistance in researching obscure historical facts and theories. My thanks to them as well.

On my own behalf and that of the School of American Research, I offer sincere thanks to the businesses and individuals who made generous contributions toward the publication costs for this book: John and Renee Benjamin, Peter Dechert, Barbara Erdman, La Fonda, Owen M. Lopez, Gerald Peters, Claire L. Phillips, Sunwest Bank of Santa Fe, and Charles Venrick.

INTRODUCTION

> I founded a villa on the banks and in the valley of the Rio del
> Norte in a good place as regards land, water, pasture, and fire-
> wood. . . .The church is done; it is very capacious and decent.
> . . .The other houses for the settlers are finished, with their cor-
> rals and irrigation ditches in place and the water running. The
> fields are sown; everything is in good order, and there has been
> no expense to the royal treasury. (Hackett 1937:379)

This quotation, from a Certificate of Founding addressed to the King of
Spain in 1706, commemorates the first days of a village in the frontier
colony of New Mexico. Between the founding of San Gabriel in 1598
and the end of the Mexican era in 1846, Spanish and Mexican colonists
settled many such villages. Their beginnings have been documented
through the journals and papers of explorers and priests, among others,
but the villages as they exist today are less clearly understood. Few people are aware of the similarities they bear to the villages of the past or
how they have changed in response to twentieth-century life.

Most of these villages lie in the north-central part of the state along
the river banks and in the mountain valleys. Defined by a clustering of
houses and outbuildings in the vicinity of a village church, they share
a common cultural background. The people, who originally banded
together for mutual defense, continue to enjoy economic, religious, and
social benefits from their association. Populations vary from one man
or one family living in what was once a vital settlement to villages of
one thousand or more. The numbers fluctuate as some people leave to
find jobs and others return home to retire. Today, many villages are
ghost towns, where empty buildings serve as reminders of the past.

During the past four hundred years, these settlements have survived under the governments of Spain, Mexico, and the United States.

They exist today in spite of devastating attacks by nomadic Indians, a Pueblo Indian rebellion, drought, disease, poverty, and an isolation so severe that it allowed aspects of seventeenth-century Spain and Mexico to survive to the present day.

In the years since Mexican sovereignty, these small towns have been increasingly exposed to outside influences, and little by little, they have evolved a unique culture. A few villages have grown into large, anglicized cities, but even those hidden away in mountain valleys or far from the highway on a difficult dirt road have become at least partially absorbed into the Anglo lifestyle. They now depend on the outside world for most of their material needs. But while Anglo concepts and values have been adapted to the Spanish lifestyle, the people's pride in their past has allowed many of the old traditions to survive. The villages are now a unique blend of two worlds.

The photographs in this book offer a brief glimpse into the Hispanic village today—the people and their way of life. They were taken in many different villages in northern and central New Mexico from 1973 to 1985. Even within this brief time, many of the buildings and customs pictured here have disappeared.

CHAPTER ONE

HISTORY

The Kingdom of New Mexico began as a lonely outpost of Spanish civilization—the northernmost settlement of the viceroyalty of New Spain. The Spanish Crown wanted to expand its dominion to the north, thereby gaining access to a new source of mineral wealth and protecting the rich mining areas of Mexico from Indian attack. Northern colonization was also viewed as a new opportunity for Franciscan priests to convert the Indians to Catholicism.

In 1595, Felipe II, King of Spain, authorized the new settlement and contracted with Don Juan de Oñate, a wealthy and prestigious citizen of New Spain, to lead the expedition. He was to equip and lead a caravan of soldiers, priests, and colonists into what was a largely unknown area of potentially hostile natives. Authorized to conquer and pacify New Mexico, Oñate was advised that his "main purpose shall be in the service of God our Lord, the spreading of His holy Catholic faith, and the missionizing of the natives of the said provinces" (Samora and Simon 1977:41).

The colonists and soldiers traveling with Oñate came mostly from Spain and Mexico. They carried with them the character and customs of sixteenth-century Spain as well as the Spanish-Mexican culture that had evolved from seventy-five years of colonization in New Spain.

The trip took six months. They traveled by horse, in ox carts, and on foot, taking the essentials for survival with them. With eighty-three wagonloads of supplies and several thousand head of stock, the 129 soldier-colonists, their families, and ten Franciscan friars were able to cover only five to six miles a day. Journeying across deserts and deep arroyos and around mountains and mesas, they were plagued by heat and thirst. But the Pueblo Indians were friendly and offered no resistance to colonization. In the late summer of 1598, near the confluence of the Rio Grande and the Chama River, the long journey ended and they established the first European village in New Mexico.

Life was difficult on the northern frontier. Until 1608, harsh weather and a scarcity of food forced the colonists to depend upon the resources of the Pueblo Indians. By 1610, other groups of settlers had arrived, and slowly, scattered ranches and small homesteads were established along the northern and central Rio Grande watershed. Many of the colonists, remembering life in similar arid areas of Spain and Mexico, knew how to survive in this kind of environment. Combining this knowledge with skills borrowed from the local Indians, they built their homes of adobe brick, stone, and timber from the nearby mountains. They constructed intricate irrigation systems, some of which still exist today. They planted crops, grazed their sheep in vast open ranges, and instituted a way of life which, while bound by Spanish law, was suited to their needs.

The colony proved disappointing as a producer of wealth, but the Pueblo Indian missions justified its continued existence as a province. The policy of the viceroyalty of New Spain towards the Pueblos had always been one of protection and control rather than assimilation or destruction. But in spite of laws that guaranteed their just treatment, the Indians were often mistreated and exploited. They were expected to pay tribute, and they were used for heavy labor. Although the Franciscan missionaries sought to convert them to Christianity and to protect them from the harsh treatment of the soldiers, they also tried to suppress ancient Indian beliefs. Eventually, hatred replaced tolerance, and in 1680 the Pueblos united in a rebellion of such fury that it forced the Spaniards from New Mexico.

They did not reconquer the region until 1693. In August of 1692, Captain General Diego de Vargas marched up the Rio Grande Valley with a small army, accepted the submission of the Pueblos, and made promises of better treatment. In 1693 he returned with colonists to reoccupy the capital city of Santa Fe.

This was a new beginning. The colony had to be rebuilt on a different basis—exploitation of the Indian, while always illegal, was no longer tolerated. Many new settlers joined the original colonists who had returned with de Vargas, and a system of land grants was initiated to provide for the expanded population. During this period, life in the frontier settlements was often a grim struggle to survive because of unrelenting raids by hostile nomadic Indian tribes and continued isolation from the outside world. By the late eighteenth century, the colony was almost totally ignored by weakening political and religious authorities in the Spanish Empire, and the people were forced to provide for themselves.

Eighteenth-century New Mexico was characterized by slow, gradual growth. People settled in clusters of individual ranches and small plazas, many of them fortified against Indian attack, with adjacent fields for crops, nearby grazing lands for cattle and sheep, and always, a church —the emotional center of the village. Folk artists fashioned religious images of saints in their own unique manner, and by the end of the Spanish era, the *Penitente* brotherhood, a lay religious order, had evolved to fill the void left by departing Spanish friars.

To a large extent, horses and guns were responsible for the Spanish conquest of the Southwest. The Indians had only stone-tipped weapons for warfare. By 1640, however, the Apaches and other nomadic tribes had become armed horsemen of exceptional skill, sweeping down on the exposed herds and settlements of the Spaniards, killing settlers and taking captives. Despite periods of relative calm, the colonial settlements were islands in the midst of chaos. They were surrounded on all sides by hostile tribes of Navajos, Utes, Comanches, and Apaches. At times the raids became so intense that Spanish expansion became impossible, and in spite of defensive tactics and retaliatory raids, the nomads were never completely subdued during the Spanish period.

Perhaps the single most significant aspect of the Spanish colonial period in New Mexico was isolation. For more than two centuries, the people were largely cut off from the European world by geography, Spanish exclusionary policies, and hostile Indians. Forbidding mountains, deserts, and plains surrounded the colony on all sides. Travel was difficult, with no waterways or roads to ease the journey. The colonists had only *carretas*, carts pulled by oxen or horses, to haul their loads. Their only regular contacts with the outside world were with trade caravans that regularly traveled the fifteen hundred miles to Chihuahua, Mexico, over the *Camino Real*, returning with supplies and new colonists. In addition, the Spanish government felt that excessive interest from outsiders might lead to a confrontation over ownership of the province and closed its borders to foreign trade or exploration. But more than anything else, the danger of attack from nomadic Indian tribes confined the colonists to their settlements, often preventing them from traveling back and forth between their own villages. Isolated from each other as well as from the outside world, they were left to their own resources, scarcely touched by changes or new trends in Europe or New Spain. With no stimulus to change the only values and customs they knew, the colonists held to their traditional ways. Out of this isolation came a new and unique culture—a blend of Spanish, Mexican, and Pueblo Indian characteristics. Based on the old values, it was a lifestyle adapted to current needs.

In 1821, after years of struggle, Mexico broke away from the crumbling Spanish Empire and formed an independent nation. The far northern villages were now a part of Mexico and for the next twenty-five years came under the jurisdiction of Mexican authorities. Because of internal discord in Mexico City, the region was again neglected and often ignored. Although the northern province felt little political change during the period of Mexican sovereignty, it began to breach two centuries of isolation. Mountain men followed the waterways of northern New Mexico in search of beaver. The Santa Fe Trail joined New Mexico to the United States. For the first time, foreigners were allowed to live and trade within New Mexico. Besides inexpensive manufactured goods, things the settlers had always done without, they brought new ideas and influences with them. Some of the villages, which had changed little during the Spanish period because of the lack of outside contacts, were suddenly exposed to an influx of strangers. It was the beginning of a new era for the frontier villages, one that would gradually change their lifestyle and values.

Under Mexican rule, the Spanish system of granting land to new communities continued to accommodate an ever-expanding population, and despite danger from nomadic Indians, people began moving outward from the Rio Grande Valley to adjacent areas in increasing numbers. Settlement of the sheltered canyons of the Pecos River Valley extended to the edge of the eastern plains, and to the north, immigrants from Taos moved across the mountains into the Mora and San Luís valleys. Soon, virtually every irrigable area in northern and central New Mexico supported small ranches and villages.

New Mexico was occupied by the United States in 1846, and its people became United States citizens. Although the Treaty of Guadalupe Hidalgo guaranteed protection of civil and property rights, the superiority and arrogance of Anglos who saw the adobe villages as composed of "miserable mud houses" (Davis 1857:35) and the customs as "picturesque medievalism or savagery" (L. Bloom 1936:274) bred hostility and bitterness on the part of many Hispanos. Application of United States property laws threatened the Spanish and Mexican land grants and resulted in the loss of many areas to Anglo encroachers. Military garrisons were established by the newcomers in an effort to control the Plains Indians, whose attacks on the villages had increased during the chaos of war and changing governments. This was the first real protection the villages had enjoyed, but the hostile Indians were not finally defeated until the late 1870s. In 1879 the first transcontinental railroad entered the territory in spite of opposition by some New Mexicans who thought it "would disturb old customs and destroy their way of life"

(Ream 1980:92). The railroad had a powerful influence on the economy of what had been a remote and inaccessible area. New towns sprang up, mining industries prospered, and new products such as canned goods, glass windows, and metal for roofs were imported into the area from the eastern United States.

Travelers of other ethnic backgrounds also began to arrive in greater numbers. These Americans brought with them a different economic outlook—a commercial system radically different from the Hispanic, self-contained, agrarian way of life. The traditional subsistence and barter economy was gradually replaced by one based on cash, with a dependence on outside markets to supplement production.

During the early years of the occupation, assimilation of the new lifestyle was slowed considerably by several factors. Unfamiliar customs, the arid landscape, and danger from hostile Indians discouraged Anglos from wanting to settle in New Mexico. And the distrust and fear that many Hispanos felt for their conquerers led them to retreat, as much as possible, to their villages and cling to their familiar way of life.

By the early twentieth century, Hispanos were being faced with the loss of much of their common lands, and their rapidly increasing population saw what remained divided and subdivided with each generation until individual plots of irrigable land were too small to support a family. Along with the loss of the traditional economy, this fragmentation forced men to leave the villages and find work as day laborers on the railroad or in the mines. Hispanos became increasingly dependent on the national economy for jobs that would support the new lifestyle. During the Great Depression, with no outside jobs, the men returned to the villages, barely surviving on faming and occasional work relief projects. It was no longer possible to exist solely on the old methods of subsistence. Too many things had changed.

Since World War II, many Hispanic people have left the villages to work elsewhere. For those who have remained, contemporary village life is apt to be characterized by low wages or welfare payments. Educational and employment opportunities have broadened in recent years, but hardship and poverty often persist. Still, some villages survive. They have emerged into the late twentieth century, accepting that which is necessary for survival in today's world but retaining many values from the past.

Portrait, Mora Valley, New Mexico.

CHAPTER TWO

THE PEOPLE

The interweaving of elements from many racially distinct groups resulted in the unique lifestyle that developed in the mountains and deserts of New Mexico. Some of the colonists came directly from Spain, but others were natives of New Spain—mostly mestizos of Spanish-Mexican descent, some Mexican Indians, and a few blacks. Eventually, continued contact with the Pueblo and Plains tribes of the Southwest added another dimension to the mixture. Soon, native-born people of mixed blood predominated in the local population, and by 1800 it was estimated that of the twenty thousand Hispanic citizens in New Mexico, only several hundred were wholly of Spanish ancestry (Meinig 1971:14).

This composite of racial traits and diverse cultural institutions, tempered by the effects of isolation and hardship, has survived surprisingly intact for nearly four centuries. Today, the term "Hispano" is often used to distinguish this group of Spanish-speaking New Mexicans from those of Anglo or Indian background. Although Hispanic people sometimes tend to claim Spanish ancestors while ignoring Mexican and Indian roots, most are a product of the fusion of all these ancestries.

Formerly the largest cultural group in the state of New Mexico, Hispanos were reduced to less than half the population by the influx of outsiders in the 1930s. By 1960 they constituted twenty-eight percent of the total population, and by 1980, while remaining the dominant racial group in most of the small towns and villages of northern and central New Mexico, they still represented only thirty-six percent of the state's total population.

Contemporary Hispanos display cohesion as a group. They have become a strong political force, increasingly assuming leadership roles in directing their own future. Today, many are determined to retain their cultural identity in the face of the dominant Anglo society. Certain aspects of Hispanic tradition—language and many religious customs, for example—have persisted largely because of the continued isolation of many villages, the discrimination the inhabitants have suffered, and limited educational opportunities, all of which lessened contact with the outside world and allowed traditional ways to survive. The level of education attained by today's young people is higher than that of their parents. They are finding increased opportunities for well-paid jobs in the cities, leaving many of the small towns stripped of their youth. Some people prefer village life and will endure hardship in order to stay. But poverty and boredom often breed frustration or anger, particularly in the men, and the local bars are sometimes places of violence and despair. Crimes of passion are common in counties heavily populated by Hispanos. A shooting, seemingly a traditional way of reacting to humiliation, often begins a cycle of vengeance.

But it is religion, the foundation of village life, that shows most clearly in the faces and actions of the people. Their faith has taught them humility and love, and they have learned to face hardship with

Portrait, La Manga, New Mexico.

Portrait, La Manga, New Mexico.

Portrait, Bernal, New Mexico.

dignity. A person's identity is closely tied to his family and place of birth, and his emotional ties to the village are strong. The family, while no longer operating as a complete economic unit, continues to provide social and emotional support. Often, family and community are still valued more highly than individualism.

Old people command respect in the villages. They are consulted and cared for. Their faces reflect serenity and strength. But one often sees confusion in the eyes of the teenagers, who sometimes seem torn between the excitement and promise of the large cities and the familiar values of their Hispanic small-town background.

One of the most engaging characteristics of the village people is their subtle sense of humor. With equal ease, they can make a joke about "gringo" outsiders or poke fun at themselves. They are reserved and wary with strangers, but once you are accepted, the village becomes your home too.

Portrait, Abeytas, New Mexico.

Portrait, Mora Valley, New Mexico.

Portrait, La Manga, New Mexico.

Portrait, Cleveland, New Mexico.

Portrait, Cleveland, New Mexico.

Portrait, La Manga, New Mexico.

Portrait, Cleveland, New Mexico.

Portrait, La Manga, New Mexico.

Deserted family chapel near Manuelitas, New Mexico.

CHAPTER THREE

THE CHURCH

Hispanic New Mexico is firmly anchored in the Catholic religion. For almost four centuries, the Church, while providing leadership and spiritual guidance, has been a dominant and unifying force affecting many other aspects of life. The color and pageantry of the Catholic Mass relieve the routine of life in an isolated village and console people in times of trouble. It is a religion oriented to the needs and pleasures of the whole family, and most of the major events and social occasions in the life of the villagers center around the church—baptisms, marriages, fiestas, burials. Everyone participates. Fathers carry toddlers on their shoulders during a fiesta procession. A teenage boy assists the matriarch of the village to her seat in the church. No home is without a crucifix, a statue of a saint, or a religious picture. The saints are considered part of the family and are treated with affection and familiarity.

In the past few decades, old religious traditions such as the blessing of the irrigation ditch have been neglected or discarded as lifestyles have changed. But along a village road, *descansos* still mark the resting places of past funeral processions. On a distant hill stands a tall, weathered cross—the *Calvario* (Calvary) of the local Penitente Brothers.

New Mexico's earliest churches were monumental earth forms. Patterned after the fortress-style missions in Mexico, they had flat roofs and a rectangular plan. The Spanish friars, faced with the limitations of building materials such as river rock for the foundation, adobe brick for the walls, and handhewn logs to support the earthen roof, reduced the more elaborate Mexican style to its essentials. Massive buttresses, which visually soften the shape of a church, were often added to strengthen a wall or protect it from water erosion. Windows were limited to a few, small, high-set openings, imposing little strain on the walls and preserving their insulating qualities while also giving protection from Indian arrows. When available, sheets of mica or selenite filled the spaces between wooden spindles set into the openings. Architectural elaboration was usually limited to a clerestory window, an ingenious overhead

Chapel known as la Capilla de Santo Niño, La Manga, New Mexico.

opening that dramatically channeled a flood of natural light down onto the altar; decorative beam-supporting corbels; or an ornamental parapet or arched belfry made of adobe. Fortress-style churches were built throughout the seventeenth and eighteenth centuries in Indian pueblos and Spanish towns with minor variations such as a cruciform plan in the villages and a single nave in the pueblos. Many of these structures survive today, and despite periodic remodeling and repairs, they retain an elemental sculptural quality that dominates the surrounding village and landscape.

The Pueblo Rebellion brought damage and destruction to most of the existing missions, which were either torn down or burned as Indians purged the area of visible reminders of the conquerers. When the Spaniards reoccupied the province in 1693, they instituted a program of rebuilding and new construction to accommodate the expanded population. Throughout the eighteenth century, many new villages were established, each with its church. The fortress style continued, but the quality of workmanship declined noticeably. Adobe walls were thinner and somewhat uneven, and ornamental woodwork was less skillful. There was also a sharp increase in the use of buttresses on outside walls, perhaps a reflection of poorer craftsmanship (Kubler 1972:139–40). The church at Córdova, built in 1821, has a three-foot-high adobe *banco* (earthen bench) running the length of an interior perhaps built to serve as an inside buttress for added strength or to absorb moisture from the vulnerable north wall (Brown 1978:215).

At the end of the Spanish era and throughout the years of Mexican control, the religious affairs of the territory disintegrated. The few secular priests under the jurisdiction of the Bishop of Durango, who had

Abandoned church in the once-active mining town of Márquez, New Mexico.

*Church of San José de Gracia, Las Trampas, New Mexico. More than two
hundred years old, this church is one of the best remaining examples of
Spanish colonial architecture.*

replaced the Franciscans, could not meet the needs of the population.
The little rural chapels, usually small versions of the large, fortress-style
structures, were often left unattended and decaying, and in most villages, there was no one to baptize babies or comfort the dying. During
this period, a lay religious group commonly known as the Penitente
Brotherhood emerged to fill the void created by the scarcity of priests.

The United States occupation of 1846 brought about changes in
mission architecture. The newcomers saw "the simple mud churches as
unworthy houses of worship" (Bunting 1976:102) and imposed their
own style of building on the Southwest. Pitched roofs of tin or cor-
rugated iron were built over the old earthen roofs to control leakage,
spires replaced traditional bell towers, and window openings were

enlarged and glazed. The latter practice tended to weaken adobe walls and hasten their collapse (Dickey 1949:202). Nevertheless, eighteenth-century flat-roofed buildings did not disappear completely. In some villages the style persisted in a somewhat modified and less monumental version, and since the early twentieth century, there has been a return to the fortress-style building of the Franciscans.

No tradition of graveyard art existed in New Mexico during the Spanish colonial and Mexican periods. Despite opposition from the Church's hierarchy, the dead were sometimes buried beneath the dirt floor of the church to prevent Indian desecrations. A person's status or wealth often dictated the location of burial—the higher the status, the closer to the altar. No markers were used, and often, no permanent records were kept of exactly where a body lay. The church itself served as a collective monument for everyone. In time, bodies were buried outside in the churchyard, and later, in a *camposanto* (graveyard) some distance from the church.

During the late nineteenth century, American traders introduced hand tools into the area, and for the first time, villagers obtained saws, planes, and axes for decorative woodworking. Plain wooden crosses were soon followed by decorative grave fences, shaped stone tablets, and ornate variations of the cross. Styles that were specific to a single

Old mission church, Lucero, New Mexico.

Interior, chapel in Mora County, New Mexico. The Cristo was carved many years ago by a local santero.

village or area became evident, particularly during the early twentieth century. Where an outcropping of slate or red sandstone provided easily available material, the camposanto was filled with monuments of local stone. In another village, grave markers might incorporate a unique design element—a stylized flower etched or painted onto the surface of a stone slab or a wooden cross carved in a particular style. Such localized designs could be attributed to a single craftsman or a local fashion of the time. Each village cemetery has its own special character, reflecting the local resources and the creativity of the people.

Flowers have always been an important part of village graveyards. By the end of the nineteenth century, paper flowers were being made with scraps of colorful wallpaper or advertising materials, but they faded in the sun and lost their shape in the first heavy rain. In the late 1940s, they were replaced by commercial plastic imitations, which retain their bright colors for years, accounting for the phenomenon of continuous blooms—even in the snow.

In recent years, handmade markers of individual design have become popular, often utilizing found objects. Commercial marble monuments and mortuary crosses are found among handmade concrete slabs embedded with marbles, colored glass, or old car parts arranged in decorative designs. Steel chain is welded into the shape of a headstone, and plastic saints or photographs of the deceased are encased behind glass in the center of a cross. Some of the more interesting contemporary monuments are hand-sculpted figures—a life-sized Christ figure with realistically red blood pouring from his wounds, or a sorrowing woman holding a gilt rosary in her hands. The elaborately carved wooden cross that was so popular early in the twentieth century is becoming rare. Today, the mediums are concrete and plaster.

In the spring of 1975, a shadowy image of Christ appeared on the wall of an old church building in the small town of Holman. The vision was revealed at night by the combination of uneven plaster and oblique lighting from a nearby streetlight. Some people saw nothing. For others, it was a miracle, a message from God. Hundreds of people crowded into the little town to see the wall. A few local residents took advantage of the crowds and sold hamburgers, candy, and orange bumper stickers proclaiming, "I Have Seen The Wall." Despite this touch of commercialism, the mood was quiet and reverent. A small shrine, set up at the base of the wall, held rosaries and prayer offerings left by people who came to pray for the miracle of healing. Although the crowds in Holman have almost disappeared, similar miraculous apparitions have appeared in other towns. The outline of a human figure holding what seemed to be a cross was seen on an old painted door in La Joya, and in the town of

Lake Arthur in southern New Mexico, an image of the face of Christ was found on a tortilla. Hispanic villagers, accepting the mystery of the unexplainable, believe that God still performs His miracles, even in the twentieth century.

New Mexico's traditional religious art developed during the late eighteenth century in response to the need for religious images in the villagers' homes and churches. Isolation from artistic traditions in other parts of the Spanish Empire, and the austere, simple life of the northern frontier, similar to that of sixteenth-century Spain, allowed medieval spiritual values to persist. The formality and humanistic tendencies of the baroque style of art, current in Europe and New Spain, were replaced with the simpler, idealistic expression of religious folk art (Wroth 1982). Drawing on their memories of old Spanish prototypes and influenced by wood engravings from Mexico, the early *santeros*, makers of religious images, combined personal vision, wood-carving skills, and a style characterized by economy of form and abstracted idealism. They became masters at portraying the emotion of the Crucifixion or the sorrow in a saint's eyes. Intended as symbols to aid their religious devotions, *bultos* (statues) and *retablos* (painted boards) portrayed not only the image and sacred qualities of the holy person

El Cerrito, New Mexico.

Interior, church of San José de Gracia, Las Trampas, New Mexico. The pews are a late addition, but the hand-hewn floor boards and the cross-bar candelabrum are part of the original construction.

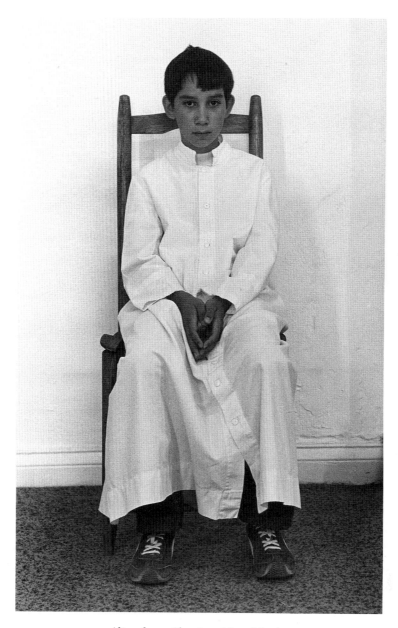

Altar boy, Abeytas, New Mexico.

but also the facial features and attitudes of the Spanish villagers themselves. The santeros imbued their images with the black hair, thin,
ascetic faces, and piety common in their own families and neighbors.
The costumes and other accouterments of the images are often of a distinctively southwestern colonial style, distinguishing them from European renderings of the same saint (Dickey 1949:169). In some areas, village workshops may have produced religious art on a large scale, as the

Hand-carved, hand-painted altar rail, Santuario, Chimayo, New Mexico.

Grave marker, Cebolla, New Mexico.

guild system did in Mexico (Wroth 1982:71), while other accounts speak of itinerant santeros who, after serving an apprenticeship, traveled through the villages making and repairing religious images for the homes, churches, and *moradas*, Penitente meeting houses. It was felt that "the better the personal and religious life of the santero, the more merit there was to be found in a specimen of his work" (Wallrich 1951:155, 160).

With the coming of the railroad to New Mexico, inexpensive religious lithographs and plaster statues began to appear in the Hispanic communities. Because the people felt that the actual *santo*, a carved or painted image of a saint, was not as important as what it represented, the santero tradition began a slow decline as many of the old, hand-carved bultos were sold to collectors in exchange for a complete set of

Virgin Mary, attributed to the nineteenth-century Santo Niño Santero.

Baptism, El Cerrito, New Mexico.

plaster saints or a new tin roof for the church. Although a few santeros continued to work in the more remote villages, producing santos for the moradas for another fifty years, the quality of workmanship suffered. The early hand-adzed retablo gave way to those painted on milled lumber, and the native tempera paints were replaced by oils and enamels. Many bultos and retablos made around the turn of the century, while exhibiting the same intensity of feeling and abstract quality as the images of earlier years, were not as skillfully crafted.

The santero tradition lay almost dormant during the early part of the twentieth century. The old carved and painted santos were considered crude and unworthy by both the new Catholic religious leaders and the Anglo newcomers. Nevertheless, a renaissance in Hispanic image making had taken place by the 1920s. While rooted in the old traditions, santos made since then reflect changes in Hispanic lifestyle and culture. Many of today's bultos and retablos are made not only for devotional use in homes and churches but for sale to a wider audience, who enjoy them for their esthetic appeal. The images created for the contemporary market are interpretations of the traditional versions, and the strictly iconographic nature of the old religious themes now survives alongside humorous renderings of animals and other secular subjects. Many contemporary carvers rely on the beauty of unpainted wood,

Wedding dance. The custom of pinning paper money on the bride's and groom's clothing is being revived in some towns.

Camposanto, or cemetery, Abiquiu, New Mexico.

A descanso, or resting place for funeral parties midway between church and burial ground. Mourners placed the small crosses and stones that mark the deceased's last place of contact with the earth.

relieved in some instances by ornamental carving, while others have returned to the use of gesso and polychrome paints.

There is renewed appreciation for the old santos in many of the small villages today. Where they still exist, they are carefully cared for and protected. Because of the possibility of theft, they are no longer kept in the churches and moradas but are stored elsewhere and brought out only on special occasions. Favorite bultos have a large wardrobe of beautiful robes and jewelry made over the years by the village women. Many are very old and in poor condition. Without knowledge of contemporary restoration techniques, the villagers must often make repairs with the materials at hand. One elderly Madonna is held together with Band-Aids and electrical tape. A coat of shiny enamel paint is sometimes applied over the stained and weathered face of an old carved saint, obscuring the intentions of the santero.

Today, religion still lies at the core of village life. Spiritual values continue to provide a source of inner strength and communal unity while villagers cope with the problems of today's world, and in some towns, there is interest in restoring some of the religious traditions that have been lost in the turmoil of twentieth-century life.

*Wall in Holman, New Mexico, where an image of Christ appeared in 1975.
Made visible by a combination of uneven plaster and oblique lighting
from a street lamp, the image was believed by many to be a miracle.*

The village of El Cerrito, New Mexico. Isolated by high mesas and miles of dirt roads, it has retained many of its early characteristics.

CHAPTER FOUR

THE VILLAGE

Small, earth toned, quiet—a feeling of timelessness. These are the New Mexican villages today. Changing slowly over the years, they are still reminders of a former way of life.

Spanish and Mexican colonists gave their villages descriptive names such as Cebolleta, "a place prolific with onions," Las Nutrias, "the beavers," or Buena Vista, "beautiful view"; names commemorating important people and places in Spanish history; local family surnames such as Abeytas or Los Lunas; or the name of the village's patron saint —San Agustín, San Isidro, Santa Rita. Many of the early Spanish villages near an Indian pueblo or pueblo ruin used rough translations of the Indian word for that place, sometimes resulting in an intermingling of languages. It is believed that "Tesuque" is a Spanish corruption of the original Tewa Indian word; "Abiquiu" may be a Spanish interpretation of the Tewa name meaning "timber end town"; and "Pecos" may come from the Keresan Indian word for water (Pearce 1965:xi–xiii).

During the earliest years of the Spanish frontier colony, the limited number of people precluded the establishment of organized settlements, and except for the provincial capital of Santa Fe, seventeenth-century New Mexico had few real villages. The people preferred to live on small ranches close to the Rio Grande pueblos to take advantage of Indian labor and tribute. Also, mission churches provided religious solace. The vulnerability of these small, isolated settlements undoubtedly contributed to the success of the Pueblo Rebellion in 1680.

The number of colonists migrating to the province increased after the reconquest. To satisfy the needs of the expanded population and to encourage settlement of outlying areas as buffers against Indian attack, a system of land grants was established by the Spanish Crown and administered by *alcaldes* (governors) under colonial law. Tracts of land

Pitched-roof adobe, Old Town, Las Vegas, New Mexico.

were granted for the founding of a few towns, but most grants were made for the establishment of individual ranches and small plazas.

According to Spanish custom, the boundaries of a typical land grant were defined by landmarks such as trees or arroyos. In 1715 a petition was approved for the land bounded by the "head of the acequia [irrigation ditch] belonging to the Taos Indians on the east; the black rocks on the west; the middle road to Picuris on the south; the arroyo hondo [deep gulley] on the north" (Jenkins 1966:92). In later years, such inexact boundary definitions contributed to the loss of Hispanic land to Anglo speculators.

During the eighteenth and early nineteenth centuries, New Mexico was essentially a rural province with many small, self-sufficient communities located close to irrigable land. In spite of their vulnerability to attack, most people lived on loosely clustered individual plots close to their fields and livestock. Their homes and corrals were often built in a single compact unit called a *casa-corral*, with high walls for protection. In frontier areas such as Las Trampas or Mora, where the danger was greatest, small fortified villages were established. The rooms were built contiguously with a common windowless outside wall around a

irrigation ditch, Holman, New Mexico.

Flat-roofed adobe, El Valle, New Mexico.

small plaza, where livestock could be corraled at night or during a raid. The single entrance into the enclosure was defended with a heavy gate, and in some places, defensive towers were built for additional protection. Despite periodic devastation from the Indians, the areas of occupied land continued to increase. Small chapels were built near the homes, livestock grazed in open areas, and irrigation ditches were dug to bring water from the river to the fields.

Beginning with the period of Mexican rule and continuing into the years of United States occupation, disruptive forces brought about a gradual change in Hispanic settlement patterns. In some areas, the expanded population strained the agricultural capacity of the land, particularly during years of drought. Along with the danger of attack and the eventual loss of traditional grazing lands, this strain forced many of the isolated families to group together into organized settlements for defense and for more economical use of the land. Some of the towns existing today were formed during this period of consolidation (Snow 1979:50–51). In areas where such defense was no longer necessary, many of the fortified towns were abandoned in favor of the linear village. Here, the homes were strung out along the river or road instead of clustering around a central plaza.

Although the villages had a common heritage and shared many cultural traits, differences of geography and economy affected the lifestyle and attitudes of the inhabitants. For most of the year, mountain villages were isolated from other towns by distance and difficult terrain, causing the people to become more cohesive and self-sufficient than those in other areas. River villages had close contacts with the Pueblo Indians and the urban life of the provincial capital, and many, located along trade routes, were exposed to foreign goods and ideas (Van Ness 1979:38–39, 43). Even today, the people in these villages are more open in their dealings with outsiders.

The economy of the Hispanic villages was traditionally based on varying proportions of farming and herding. Those who had access to plots of irrigable land along the rivers placed greater importance on agriculture, while the grasslands of the plains and plateaus offered forage for raising stock. By the nineteenth century, many villages were

Pitched-roof adobe, Santa Cruz, New Mexico.

broadening their economy in response to changing conditions. The community of Tuerto, which arose in the San Pedro mountains in 1839 to supply gold miners, became a boom town with more than twenty stores (Townley 1971: 114–15). The villages of Antón Chico and Puerto de Luna are representative of the frontier towns from which *comancheros*, Hispanic traders, traveled across the plains to barter with the Comanches and other Plains tribes. For almost a century, from 1786 until the United States occupation, comancheros traded food to the Indians for livestock and buffalo skins. Wagon trains bringing immigrants and supplies from the east on the Santa Fe Trail forded the Pecos River at San Miguel del Bado, often stopping for food or repairs. Tecolote, although settled in 1824, later became one in a series of forage depots established to supply provisions to the United States Army. The remains of the old headquarters building and stables were still visible in 1940.

After the railroad reached New Mexico in 1879, a series of new towns sprang up along the tracks to provide depots and repair shops or to supply coal and water. The village of Lamy was a junction for passengers disembarking for Santa Fe, and in the late 1800s, the small mining towns of Monero and Kelly, which depended on the railroad, flourished. Villages such as these, now ghost towns, were the forerunners of today's mining industry in New Mexico.

The Treaty of Guadalupe Hidalgo guaranteed Hispanic citizens that existing Spanish and Mexican property rights would be recognized and respected. In many cases, however, the United States failed to uphold the legal rights of the people against unscrupulous land speculators, many of whom were Anglo newcomers. Few Hispanics had the money or knowledge necessary to win a lengthy battle in a United States court. During these turbulent years, many Hispanos lost their land. Some retained village land and irrigated plots but lost the use of the traditional grazing lands. No longer able to support themselves by raising sheep or cattle, they were forced to seek wage work outside the village. It was the beginning of a gradual exodus of families from the rural Hispanic towns.

Travelers to New Mexico during the late nineteenth century viewed the Hispanic villages with mixed reactions, often judging the homes to be nothing but "uninviting mud. . .hovels" (Weber 1973:72). They saw small towns built around a church-dominated plaza and fields fed by networks of irrigation ditches. They saw thick-walled adobe houses with small deep-set doors and windows, weathered log barns, and mud baking ovens in the yards. Inside the homes they found simple hand-made furnishings. In 1834 an easterner described a room in "the best house in the village":

> In one corner of [the small, square room] stood the little fire-place, like a square stove, open on two sides, and filled with small sticks of pine set upright and burning, filling the room with all heat and comfort. Round the whole room. . .was a pile of blankets, striped red and white, answering the purpose of sofas. High up on the walls were various small looking-glasses, pictures of saints, wooden images of the Saviour, and wooden crucifixes, interspersed with divers roses of red and white cambric. These, with two or three wooden benches which served for both chairs and tables, completed the furniture of the room. (Weber 1967:103)

The adobe-style architecture found in the Hispanic villages was and is one of the few distinctive regional styles in the United States. It was built by the local people of available materials in a style adapted to New

A blend of old and new along the road in Truchas, New Mexico.

Mexico's semiarid environment, and the basic design has varied little over the years. The homes were both functional and flexible. When more space was needed, the building was extended by adding another room onto the end of the existing structure. In houses of this kind, each room could function independently with its own corner fireplace and outside entrance. Eventually, some evolved into long, low buildings of multiple homes, often taking a U or L shape; or into the *plazuela*, a single-family version of the fortified village, in which contiguous rooms surrounded and enclosed a small courtyard.

Crosses marking the site of a fatal car accident, Chimayo, New Mexico. This is probably an extension of a custom dating back to the eighteenth century, when similar markers were placed where travelers were killed by Indian ambushes.

Customized car decoration, San José, New Mexico.

Adobe bricks are traditionally made of varying proportions of local clay, sand, and straw, mixed with water to a plastic consistency, shaped into bricks, and sun dried to rock hardness. Those made by the early Spanish settlers were normally larger than the ones made today. The walls of the old mission churches were sometimes formed by laying two bricks end to end, forming a four-foot-thick wall. Today's adobes are usually about fourteen inches long. In some areas, local stone of suitable size and shape was used for walls and foundations, while logs from the mountains were used as roof beams and to frame doors and windows. Usually the brick or rock walls were covered with adobe plaster to seal out wind and moisture.

The color of adobe varies according to the local earth pigments. In some areas, the natural presence of mica in the soil adds a sparkling glint to the walls. A visitor to New Mexico in 1885 commented on the varied colors seen in the adobe buildings: "In hue the adobe varies with the region, so that each place has literally its 'local color.' [Down] the Rio Grande it passes through all shades of brown, from a rich golden tone to a burnt sienna. In some places it looks like red sandstone and others it is a light grey" (Baxter 1885:696).

Recently, when the walls of the 150-year-old church in the village of Cleveland caved in, the people decided to rebuild it themselves the old way with walls two adobes thick and *vigas* (roof beams) brought from the nearby mountains. In a concession to modernization, the logs, after being measured and notched on the ground, were lifted to the roof by a fork lift, then rolled into place. The residents built a new bell tower for the old bell, which had been salvaged from the original church, and made a good, hard adobe plaster from an old formula calling for a mixture of three parts dirt, two parts sand, and one-half part

Room interior, La Manga, New Mexico.

Village home with old Cristos and pictures of saints.

flour. Throughout the entire rebuilding process, a plaster image of San José, the patron saint of the church, kept watch from a niche on an inside wall, lending support to the work.

With the introduction of sawmills during the territorial period, ornamental woodwork began to appear on some buildings. Many of the traditional, flat roofs in the northern mountain villages were covered with steeply pitched gabled roofs that, when built properly, protected the earthen roof and walls from moisture and provided a storage area that could be reached by an outside stairway or ladder. Later, the railroads brought in galvanized iron to replace the wooden roofs. Where lumber was not easily available, the one-story, flat-roofed building stayed popular.

Also in the territorial style are the "Peñasco doors" developed in the late 1880s. Craftsmen in the mountain villages of Chacón, Rodarte, and Peñasco, among others, created cut-out and paneled doors of extraordinary inventiveness and beauty with the use of simple hand tools and wood moldings. This indigenous folk art, which came into being after tools and milled lumber became available, flourished only as long as the isolation of the villages continued. By the early 1920s, it was a dying art.

The Hispanic villages of today are in varying stages of decay or revitalization. The village of La Manga, once thriving, recently lost its last resident. The small church is still used on feast days by former residents who return for the occasion, but the dance hall, school, and homes are deserted and in need of repair. Other villages are being kept alive by a few people who prefer to live in quiet isolation. San Augustine can be reached only over nine miles of difficult dirt roads. It has no electricity or telephones, and while many buildings are unused and disintegrating, the church is well cared for, and the old camposanto is still tended by the few families who have stayed. In the village of Tecolote, where less than half the original population remains, there is still a strong sense of community evident in the well-attended church functions and in the women's group that is rebuilding the old school house into a new community dance hall and play space for the children.

Inside village houses, old linoleum and new shag rugs cover the floors. Flowered wallpaper or colorful paint hides the unevenness of the adobe-plastered walls. While some village homes still use woodburning stoves for cooking and heat, others have converted to the convenience and expense of propane gas. Most of the drafty backyard outhouses have been replaced with modern indoor plumbing, and water now comes from a village water tank instead of the river or a hand-dug well. Traditional handmade pine furniture, built for the early homes, has been mostly replaced with sturdy factory-made chairs and comfortable, over-stuffed couches. But the focal point of the home is always a table top or shelf where a colorful display of plaster saints and religious pictures accompanies a collection of family photographs. With obvious love and pride, they commemorate family milestones—from a small color snapshot of the newest baby to the faded, formal picture of the grandparents' wedding day.

Smaller and more isolated villages make fewer concessions to twentieth-century living than do the larger towns, partly because they lack commercial enterprise, but also because they are more likely to be populated by older people who prefer to cling to the traditional ways. But overall, the village profile is slowly changing. Television antennas now balance on old tin roofs, pickup trucks have long since taken over the duties of the horse-drawn wagon, and house trailers are replacing the quiet beauty of many old adobe homes. While cows and goats still wander the dirt roads and the fragrance of burning piñon hovers over the villages on cold, still nights, the increasing acceptance of modern life is changing their appearance. The surviving towns are those that have found a compromise between the old and the new, combining the disparate values of modern plumbing and old santos into a new kind of village.

Sign posted by Hispanic activists near Tierra Amarilla, New Mexico. In 1967, a group of rural Hispanics organized an unsuccessful raid on the Tierra Amarilla courthouse as part of an attempt to publicize the poverty resulting from their loss of grazing lands. The legend on the hand-printed poster, "Land or Death," indicates the intensity of their feelings.

The Rio Chama near its confluence with the Rio Grande.

CHAPTER FIVE

THE LANDSCAPE

[Man] is all that he sees; all that flows to him from a thousand sources, half noted, or noted not at all except by some sense that lies too deep for naming. He is the land, the lift of its mountain lines, the reach of its valleys.
—Mary Austin, *The Land of Journey's Ending*

Hispanic villagers are the inheritors not only of their Spanish, Mexican, and Indian ancestors but also of their surroundings. The physical attributes and spiritual qualities found in the varied landscapes of New Mexico are reflected by the people themselves, in their human qualities and their artistic and material expressions.

The villages are isolated against many different backgrounds—flat, shimmering plains where tall grasses bend before the relentless wind; stretches of hot, empty land with sparse vegetation; lonely mesas and rock formations that seem to belong to another planet. Towering mountains collect snow that survives well into the hot summer, giving birth to clear streams and winding rivers, sending life-giving water to the parched land below.

It is a landscape whose moods may change with unexpected swiftness. The fierce, obliterating blizzard gives way to a sun-sparkled, white blanket. A sudden cloudburst transforms a dry arroyo into a destructive torrent.

The sky—a gigantic stage on which many acts may be played at once. The intense blue of a summer day is the backdrop for lofty, white

Near Golondrinas, New Mexico.

clouds with undulating shapes. Over there, lightning streaks against dark thunderheads, while here, a brilliant rainbow arches over a small Hispanic village.

The dramatic and elemental nature of the New Mexican landscape is too intense for some. There is little in it that is soft or yielding. Rather, people have learned to adapt to the environment. It is a place of the spirit, where the soul finds beauty in starkness and gathers strength from the forces of nature. As one villager put it, the mountains are "an anchor. They are here. They never leave us....They are nearer God than us" (Coles 1973:34).

There is a basic psychological difference between mountain people and those who live surrounded by the wide-open spaces of the desert or plains. Villagers enclosed and isolated by mountains are often characterized as people of strong individualism, attracted to mysticism and spiritual drama, and at times, to acts of explosive reaction (Milton 1971:73, 79). The mountainous areas of northern New Mexico were the setting for the religious fervor of the early Penitentes, and in 1967, for the raid on the Tierra Amarilla courthouse by Hispanic activists.

The landscape of New Mexico—emotional geography that shapes the lives and the character of the people who live there.

Near Truchas, New Mexico.

Near Márquez, New Mexico.

Near Mora, New Mexico.

Penitente services during Holy Week.

CHAPTER SIX

LOS HERMANOS

In some of the remoter areas of northern New Mexico and southern Colorado, there exists a lay religious order known officially as *La Cofradía de Nuestro Padre Jesús Nazareno*, or more commonly, *Los Hermanos Penitentes*—the Penitente Brothers. Formed to maintain religious values and customs threatened with extinction by the scarcity of religious leaders, this brotherhood of Hispanic village men evolved during the early decades of the nineteenth century. It is thought to have been influenced in part by the lay Third Order of St. Francis. As churches disintegrated and Catholic rituals were neglected, village men organized into local chapters. Through prayer and penance, they sought to achieve a higher state of understanding and oneness with God by emulation of the Christ Spirit, including the pain and suffering of Calvary.

Penitential practices were likely to include self-flagellation, simulated crucifixions, prayers, and other devotional exercises. Throughout the Lenten season, barefoot hermanos could be seen emerging from the moradas, proceeding to a nearby Calvario. Those doing physical penance dressed in white trousers. Black hoods covered their faces to ensure humility and hide their identity from family members or other bystanders. The story is told of the small dog who ran alongside a Good Friday procession in the 1930s, barking at his Penitente master's feet and effectively revealing his identity.

In addition to their annual commemoration of the Passion of Jesus during Holy Week, the brothers have a year-round commitment to imitate His life through unobtrusive acts of charity and mutual aid, fostering by their example the ideals of Christian morality and brotherly love among the people of the villages. During the years of isolation from civil and religious authorities, they provided leadership and material aid for members and nonmembers alike, visited the sick, buried the dead, and organized wakes and rosaries. The value of the hermanos' service to their communities was incalculable, and their contributions to early village life played an important role in the survival of the traditional Hispanic lifestyle.

During the first half century of their existence, Los Hermanos functioned openly as a part of village life. Some of the rituals were open to nonmembers, and many of the earliest moradas, including those in Las Trampas and Santa Cruz, were built as an integral part of the local church. By the later part of the nineteenth century, however, the brotherhood had come into conflict with the hierarchy of the Catholic Church. New Mexican prelates criticized the brothers for the "excessive zeal" with which they carried out their penitential practices and attempted to suppress the movement (Weigle 1976:24). In the early twentieth century, Anglos who had little understanding of or regard for customs other than their own sensationalized and ridiculed the public rituals. In response to these attitudes, many moradas were moved away

Penitente morada.

Penitente morada.

from the churches to areas secluded from public view. Secrecy became a part of the Penitente rites.

As inexpensive plaster saints and mass-produced religious prints replaced the native santos in homes and churches, the major demand for handmade bultos came from the moradas, where conservative brothers held fast to their traditional ways. Thus, most of the images made during the late nineteenth century are those of central importance

Penitente morada.

Often difficult to distinguish from other village buildings, many have the look of small chapels; others might resemble a village home. Building materials differ from area to area according to the availability of local to the hermanos, images of Christ and the Virgin as they relate to the Passion: Our Father Jesus (*Nuestro Padre Jesús*), patron and namesake of the brotherhood; Christ Buried (*Cristo Entierro*); Christ Crucified (*Cristo Crucificado*); Our Lady of Sorrows (*Nuestra Señora de los Dolores*); and Our Lady of Solitude (*Nuestra Señora de la Soledad*) (Wroth 1979:281). The physical wounds depicted on the carved *Cristos* offer evidence of the early Penitentes' attempt to identify with Christ's suffering. The abstracted cuts and abrasions correspond accurately to what might result on human flesh from the penitential practices observed and recorded during the early part of the twentieth century (Mills and Grove 1956:18).

The morada is usually found in an isolated area on the edge of a village. Built specifically as meetinghouses for Penitente worship, they are constructed according to the needs and wealth of their members.

resources. The plan of a morada varies from a rectangle to more elaborate L, T, or cross shapes. Some were built with a church-style contracted chancel at one end. The roofs are flat or steeply pitched board-on-board or galvanized iron; they often support a wooden bell tower decorated with a small cross. A heavy rope extending through the ceiling allows the bell to be rung from inside.

The village morada can often be identified by its distinctively small and unobtrusive windows and doors, particularly in older structures. For privacy, the few windows—generally one to a room—are heavily curtained or covered with boards or shutters. Doors are often low, causing one to bend into a prayerful attitude when entering. One old morada in Mora County has a small, square, wood-framed opening built low into an otherwise blank wall leading to an inside room, presumably for delivering food to the sequestered brothers during Holy Week.

The cross, which plays a central role in the liturgy of the Penitentes, is more frequently associated with moradas than with churches. A tall, standing, wooden cross, often six to eight feet high, is usually located near the entrance to the morada, and on a nearby hill,

Penitente morada.

Penitente morada.

a Calvario cross stands isolated against the sky. *Maderos,* heavy wooden crosses traditionally used in Penitente processions, are sometimes found stacked against an outside wall. They can be identified by extensive wear on one side of the bottom end, caused by repeated dragging over rough terrain. Smaller crosses are seen painted on wooden doors and adobe walls or incised into rock walls, and at least one morada door has been decorated with a cross made from pieces of wood molding.

Typically, a morada has three rooms: a chapel, or *oratorio;* a meeting room used for congregating, eating, and sleeping; and a room for storing maderos and other equipment used in penitential rituals. Older buildings have floors of hard-packed dirt or rough planks. The walls are whitewashed or painted in subdued colors. One deserted morada, said to date from the late 1800s, has remnants of flowered wallpaper clinging to the crumbling adobe walls. The rooms are heated by cast-iron stoves, a corner fireplace, or occasionally by an oil-drum stove. In some moradas, the chapel is left unheated; only the meeting room has a stove.

The most important room, and generally the one with the best furnishings, is the chapel. Across one end of the room, an altar, crowded

Penitente morada.

Penitente morada.

with candles, crosses, and images of Christ and the Virgin, is framed with a lace or embroidered valance or with decoratively cutout plywood. Modern commercial statues share the altar with nineteenth-century hand-carved Cristos and Madonnas wearing beautiful clothes. Sometimes the chapel has a handmade altar rail, banners, or a large, triangular candelabrum. The rest of the room is generally bare except for a few benches or chairs and some framed religious pictures on the wall.

The meeting room is furnished with a table, benches, and perhaps an old cupboard. Because many moradas have no electricity, a kerosene lantern may hang from a ceiling beam. The meeting-room fireplace or wood stove, which heats the room during cold weather, is also used to warm food for the brothers during an extended retreat or the Lenten meals served during Holy Week.

Built for prayer and penance, moradas are sparsely furnished. Luxuries are neither needed nor wanted. Furnishings are usually brought from the brothers' homes or salvaged from the local church when it was last remodeled. Benches and tables are unadorned and often hand-made. The curtains are sewn and washed by the women of the village. Wooden floors are swept clean, and those of hard-packed earth are sprinkled periodically with water to keep the dust down.

Today, the New Mexico landscape is dotted with the shells of once-active moradas. Some have been torn down and salvaged for building materials. In one village, the last active morada has only two brothers left, both older men, keeping the traditional beliefs alive. On certain occasions, men from moradas in nearby towns join them in their rituals. The young people of the village have not become Penitentes because "it is so hard" to devote one's life to prayer, penance, and exemplary

Unusual cutout plywood frame for a morada altar.

Altar, Penitente morada.

Christian behavior. In another town, a father advised his son not to get involved because "the way a Penitente has to live is so difficult, and if you can't live like that, you shouldn't do it at all."

Nevertheless, the brothers are still active in many areas and in some cases have increased their membership. Many of the old moradas are being rebuilt, and the ancient rites are being taught to a new generation of initiates. A morada in Mora County, built in 1908, stood empty after 1940, when the men went off to defense-related jobs in distant states, but was reopened in 1975, with a Mass celebrated by a local priest. The men who returned have slowly remodeled and furnished the building, and today the membership includes both young and old.

The practice of self-flagellation, common in the early years, has been replaced by penance of a milder nature. What goes on in a morada during Holy Week is private, but recent accounts name prayers and fasting as the current means of commemorating the Passion of Christ. Yet in the dim, predawn light of a recent Good Friday, barefoot hermanos were glimpsed slowly dragging heavy maderos along the path to Calvary.

Altar, Penitente morada. An old bulto stands alongside a modern religious statue.

Each morada has its own traditions. Some practice simple religious ceremonies, others have elaborate dramatizations of the Passion dating back to the nineteenth century. The Good Friday observance in one morada was highlighted by a three-o'clock procession along the *Via Crucis*—the Way of the Cross. The brothers and their friends walked slowly along a path from the morada to the Calvario cross on a nearby hill, kneeling at *estaciones* to pray the fourteen stations of the cross. The

*Penitente brother holding an old bulto of Maria
Santísima, made by the santero José Benito Ortega.*

Calvario at Gallina Plaza, New Mexico.

Penitente services during Holy Week.

procession was led by an hermano carrying a small *Sangre de Cristo* (an image of the Christ Crucified; literally, "blood of Christ"). Another Cristo was tied to a Calvario cross symbolizing the Crucifixion. The observance also included recitation of the rosary and prayers for the dead.

In another town, the hermanos observed Good Friday with the *Encuentro*, a dramatization of the encounter between Jesus and His Mother on the path to Calvary. Accompanied by the plaintive sound of *pitos*, flutelike reed instruments, brothers led the villagers to the Calvario cross in the nearby camposanto. At the head of the line they carried an almost lifesized figure of Christ, completely shrouded in black. Only the hands, tied with rope, were visible. As the column progressed along the path to Calvary, pausing at intervals to pray the stations of the cross, they were met by women from the church's Altar Society carrying an equally large figure of Mary. In a touching reenactment of their sorrow, the two bultos tilted toward one another as Mary bid farewell to her Son. The expressions and the bearing of the old Hispanic bultos mirrored the intense feelings evident in the faces of the villagers as they symbolically shared in the suffering of Christ.

In another town, Good Friday was celebrated with *Las Tres Caídas*, a dramatization of the three falls of Jesus on the road to Calvary. Brothers led the procession with a bulto of *Nuestro Padre Jesús*, followed by women from the church carrying an image of *La Madre Dolorosa*. Along the way, the villagers sang traditional *alabados* (hymns), prayed, and narrated their reenactment of the event (La Iglesia de Santa Cruz de la Cañada 1983:54).

Some years, cold winds still blow during Easter week, and snow lies in dirty patches on the frozen ground. The stations of the cross may then be said inside the morada, where the brothers kneel on a hard plank or dirt floor. But believing that Good Friday is a day of sacrifice, they will usually suffer the cold as part of their penance. They and their guests eat a meatless Lenten meal served on long tables set up in the meeting room. Groups of hermanos sing hymns, reading from small notebooks handwritten in old Spanish.

During Easter week, the morada is home for many brothers who stay there twenty-four hours a day, fasting and continuing their prayers throughout the night. The activities of Holy Week are coordinated by

Penitente services during Holy Week.

an *hermano mayor* (principal brother), who plans the processions, the stations of the cross, and ceremonies such as *Las Tinieblas*, the dramatic depiction of the darkness and earthly chaos that followed Christ's death. *Mayordomos* are appointed to oversee the preparation of food for the public and for the brothers after they have ended their fast. The women spend long hours cooking customary Lenten dishes such as egg fritters with chile or *panocha*, a sprouted-wheat pudding.

La Bajada del Santísimo de la Cruz, the lowering of Christ from the cross, is performed according to the traditions of the village. Called the *descendimiento* in some moradas, it takes place on Good Friday with an afternoon procession to the Calvario. There, a crucifix which had been tied to the cross is removed and symbolically buried. In another village, a similar event traditionally takes place on the third of May. A crucifix is placed on a small stepladder in front of the altar in the morada. The kneeling hermanos and *padrinos* (godparents) of the morada move forward in pairs. Between stanzas of the rosary, each couple in turn reaches out and lowers the crucifix one step until all the participants have been accommodated.

Penitente services during Holy Week.

For nearly 150 years, the brotherhood has persevered despite the curiosity and criticism of outsiders. In spite of the increasing numbers of abandoned moradas, in certain areas the membership has stabilized or increased. Even though the brothers' role as protectors and leaders of the village diminished as their numbers declined and many of their charitable contributions were replaced with government welfare programs, they are still a valuable asset to their communities. The estimated 2,530 hermanos active in New Mexico and Colorado in the 1980s (Bunting, Lyons, and Lyons 1983:34) continue to fulfill their avowed aims to serve God, live humbly, and act with charity and love towards one another.

Cleaning an irrigation ditch, El Cerrito, New Mexico.

CHAPTER SEVEN

MAKING A LIVING

During the colonial years, people survived by adapting methods brought with them from Spain and Mexico and by learning new methods from the Indians. Their subsistence lifestyle was based on sixteenth- and seventeenth-century cultural patterns and the uncertainties of life in a sometimes hostile environment. Trade with the outside world was sporadic and limited mostly to the wealthier families of Santa Fe and Albuquerque. For the isolated village people, barter was often the only means of economic exchange. They traded labor among themselves, building homes, harvesting crops, maintaining the community irrigation system, and protecting the village from Indian raids.

People lived on what the land could provide and made the things they needed. Tools and hardware such as iron axes, nails, and wagon wheels were imported at great cost by the more fortunate, but most villagers had to rely on handmade wooden pegs or oxen yokes fashioned from wood and rawhide. An early traveler to New Mexico spoke of huge wooden wagon wheels that were "never greased, but left to howl and groan in such a dismal way that teams unused to them are frequently frightened by the noise" (Farrar 1968:140). Except for relying on the santero and the *curandera*, a woman especially skilled at healing with herbs, most families learned to provide for themselves.

The economics of early village life was based almost entirely on noncommercial agriculture and herding. In the semiarid Southwest, the use and distribution of water has always been of vital importance. With their knowledge of irrigation practices in Spain, the settlers dammed small rivers and streams, and with handmade tools, dug networks of acequias to divert water to cultivated areas—a system similar to the ditch system being used by some Pueblos when the Spaniards arrived. The large number of irrigation-related customs and beliefs that have survived for hundreds of years—ranging from incorporated ditch associations and bylaws to religious processions with the village santos—reflect the importance of water for survival.

Blessing the water at the ditch that serves La Joya and Contreras, New Mexico.

In the early years, a family was responsible for its own ditch. But as the population grew, agricultural lands spread to areas further away from the river, the network of acequias grew, and the problems of water management became more complex, necessitating ditch associations and water-rights laws. In most Hispanic communities today, a *mayor-domo de acequia* (ditch boss) and a three-man commission are elected annually to direct the maintenance of the dam and ditches and to see that irrigation water is distributed in proportion to the land under cultivation. Every landowner with property along the ditch is entitled to a share of the water, and he is expected to help build and maintain the irrigation system. In some villages, anyone who violates the bylaws may be deprived of his right to the water until a fine is paid. In dry seasons or in areas where the acequia is shared by many families, the mayor-domo rations the water. Depending on the amount of water available and the number of potential users, each landowner is assigned specific hours when he may open the gates and let the water flow over his land. During a busy growing season, it is not unusual to see farmers irrigating their fields by flashlight in the middle of the night.

The construction of an irrigation system takes hard work and a common-sense knowledge of engineering. Dams, which channel the water into the ditch system, are usually located some distance up the river from the fields. The dams are built of native rock, branches, logs, even old car bodies, and stabilized with wire. While inexpensive, such dams require constant repairs to survive heavy flooding. In recent years, various state and federal programs have offered financial aid for building more permanent dams, but little actual help has yet been received by the villagers.

Each year in the early spring, the dam must be repaired and the ditches cleaned of any debris that would obstruct the flow of water. On the appointed day, the village men take their places in the ditch, each armed with a shovel. The mayordomo measures off each man's working space and oversees the work as it progresses. Despite the hard work, the men joke among themselves as they shovel accumulated sediment and rubble out onto the banks. As each section is cleared, the crew moves as a unit to the next segment, where the work begins again. Meanwhile, the women have been cooking, and at noon, the men return to the village to eat.

Image of San Isidro, patron saint of farmers, watching over crops at La Manga, New Mexico.

When all the ditches have been cleaned and the water is again flowing for another season's planting, a few villages such as La Joya still observe the old tradition of blessing the ditch. Accompanied by the parish priest, the people carry their santos in procession from the church to the irrigation ditch, where the priest blesses the ditch and the water. This custom is rapidly disappearing as the importance of agriculture in village life diminishes.

While activities involving the acequias have changed little over the years, many larger ditches, which once might have required several weeks to clean by hand, are now cleared with a tractor in a few days. Where money is available, some ditches are being lined with concrete for easier maintenance. Although the irrigation ditch continues to play an important role in the survival of villages like El Cerrito or Sena, it is losing its importance in others. In Tecolote, following several years of neglect, the dam is disintegrating and the ditches are filled with debris. The men in this town have little interest in repairing the irrigation system because outside jobs have made them less dependent on their crops.

After 1846, visitors to the new territory reported on the native subsistence economy and its almost total dependence on food crops and

Harvest during year of drought, La Manga, New Mexico.

Strings of red chile peppers hung to dry in the sun, San Pedro, New Mexico.

stock raising. To many Anglos, the farming implements appeared crude and primitive. The plows were nothing "but the fork of a small tree, with only one handle. The point entering the ground is sometimes shod with iron" (J. Bloom 1959:176). But with the simplest tools, Hispanic villagers produced enough food for their own survival. They had brought seed for staples such as corn and beans from Mexico, and they planted fruit trees for small orchards. Early inhabitants gathered wild herbs for seasoning and edible plants such as lamb's-quarters, asparagus, and sheep sorrel; caught fish in the rivers; and hunted for deer, beaver, and wild duck. Chokecherries were gathered along the streams, and the fall harvest of piñon nuts provided a rich, nourishing treat. Much of the food grown during the summer was preserved for the long, cold winter. Root vegetables were buried in sand, while corn, beans, chile, and fruit were sun dried. Every village home had a storeroom for hanging meat and game and storing dried foods.

Shearing a sheep in the traditional way at el Rancho de las Golondrinas, La Cienega, New Mexico.

Several varieties of corn and some wheat were ground into flour for tortillas and bread. In the early days, many villages supported small grist mills run by river water—while faster than the Indian method of grinding by hand, still a slow process. One writer states that a mill could grind only about one bushel in twenty-four hours (Frazer 1968:43–44).

Stock raising was the basis of village economy. Common lands offered adequate forage for the large numbers of stock first brought into New Mexico by Oñate, particularly the great flocks of sheep that grazed the plains and hillsides of the early colony. The sheepherder had the lonely responsibility of caring for thousands of sheep at a time, protecting them from predators and the weather. In the practice of *el partido*, which began during the days of Spanish rule and continued well into the twentieth century, independent stockmen, known as *partidarios*, contracted with large sheep owners to care for a flock of sheep over a stipulated period of time. In return, they received annual payment in the form of a percentage of the offspring and sheared wool.

Sheep were economically important as a source of food, wool, which along with some locally grown cotton was woven into cloth, and hides, which were tanned for leather. They were also used as bartering currency. In 1826 "a narrow parcel of land 20×260 yards sold for 6 sheep, 5 serapes, one handworked spread, one calf, 2½ fanegas of wheat, 5 sacks of corn, one pair fine stockings and one Pueblo belt" (Ream 1980:36).

The life of a shepherd has changed little since the last century. For most of the year, he still leads a solitary life tending his flocks, but today the white herders' tents that once dotted the countryside have been replaced by small silver trailers equipped with wood stoves and battery-powered radios. Crews of itinerant sheepshearers still travel from village

Butchering a hog, San Augustine, New Mexico.

Contemporary santero, Nambe, New Mexico.

to village to shear the larger flocks, but now they work with motor-driven shears, increasing the amount of wool they can cut in a day.

The immense flocks have declined in recent years. The loss of traditional grazing lands, competition from the growing cattle industry, and lower demand for wool with the advent of synthetic fibers have all diminished the economic importance of sheep. It was estimated that in 1950, there were more than 120,000 sheep in Rio Arriba County alone; in 1981, there were 5,000 (Casarez 1981:A-5).

In the fall and early winter, groups of ciboleros (buffalo hunters) moved out onto the great eastern plains with pack burros and carretas and hunted from horseback with only a lance to bring down the huge animals. "In 1832, it was estimated that the ciboleros were killing a minimum of ten to twelve thousand buffalo annually" (Kenner 1969:98). Dried buffalo meat cooked with chile and beans, a common dish in most homes, helped sustain the villagers through the winter.

Weaver working at a traditional treadle loom, Ledoux, New Mexico.

The village store, Chimayo, New Mexico.

By the late 1870s, the buffalo had disappeared. Lost grazing lands and the rapid growth of the new commercial lifestyle soon forced many Hispanic landowners to find jobs outside the village. This trend has continued through the twentieth century until now, in the 1980s, survival in the small, isolated villages depends largely on outside income. Some people receive welfare or retirement checks; others commute to jobs in nearby urban areas. Often, the whole family moves to the city during the work week, returning home on weekends and for vacations.

In a few of the larger villages such as Mora, Peñasco, and Chimayo, the availability of local employment explains a feeling of stability and growth. As shopping centers for more rural areas or as tourist attractions, these towns are able to provide jobs for some people. Others find work close to home with the Highway Department or a local construction company. Many older residents live on retirement pensions earned from years of working in distant mines or factories, and as in more remote villages, some people commute to work or live on welfare checks and occasional odd jobs.

Although most of the remaining villagers depend on work in the cities, a few enterprising, creative people have found ways to increase their income at home by providing needed services or producing items of artistic merit. Small general stores, gas stations, a single-window post office, and an occasional barber shop or restaurant employ local residents in some of the larger towns. In Velarde and Chimayo, roadside stands do a brisk business during the growing season, when fresh fruits and vegetables are plentiful. In the fall, the stands blaze with pumpkins, apples, and long strings of startlingly red chiles. In Córdova, wood carvers create modern versions of the saints, and Chimayo weavers produce the well-known Chimayo blanket for sale to tourists. Many of the traditional Hispanic arts and crafts are experiencing a renaissance as a result of worldwide interest in the folk arts.

General store, Chimayo, New Mexico.

During the Spanish colonial and Mexican periods, people provided their own entertainment as well as the basic necessities of life. Today, villagers continue to enjoy many of those same customs, and through them, a sense of continuity with the past.

The *matanza*, a centuries-old tradition that still functions in many villages, is a social occasion associated with the chore of butchering and preserving meat. It is traditionally held in the late fall or early winter, when the air is cool enough to retard spoilage. Recently, in San Augustine, a sheep was butchered; in La Joya, it was a pig. Friends and relatives were invited to spend the day working and socializing. The men butchered and prepared the meat while the women cooked a traditional meal. Nothing was wasted. The skin of the pig was rendered to make *chicharrones*, its intestines were used as casing for sausage, and the blood was made into a pudding. At one time, the ears would have been made into purses.

The dance hall was once an important fixture in most villages, with weekly dances attended by young and old. One woman remembers as a very small child hearing the fiddles and watching the dusty feet of the dancers from under the bench where she had been put to sleep. But

Postmistress, La Joya, New Mexico.

Wood collected for winter heating and cooking, Cleveland, New Mexico.

today, the dance halls are silent and pickup trucks take the young people to nearby cities to find entertainment.

Early Spanish colonists raced the first horses brought to New Mexico, and horse racing is still a popular Hispanic sport. Trucks have replaced horses in most villages, but many men continue to take pride in their horsemanship. Today's race is often held on short notice. While some races are called for breaking in a new horse to the track, most are challenge races—one man and his horse against another. The challenger bets money or perhaps a case of beer on his horse, and the spectators wager actively among themselves. The track, a narrow, graded area in an isolated field, is sometimes equipped with a two-horse gate at one end. The spectators line the track with their cars and trucks, and often a local family will sell cokes or *burritos*. People may wait several hours for the event to begin, but the actual race lasts for only one length of the track.

During the nineteenth and early twentieth centuries, itinerate puppeteers traveled from village to village with *titeres*, or handmade marionettes. A portable stage was set up in the local dance hall. Many puppeteers were skilled at managing the voices and movements of several

*Replastering the church and repainting the bell tower, a community
effort at Abeytas, New Mexico.*

Impromptu horse race in northern New Mexico.

puppets at once. Records from the 1830s state that some scripts were loosely based on the writings of Cervantes and other Spanish writers. Later accounts indicate that dramatic stories based on contemporary life had become popular. *Los Titeres* continued as a favorite form of entertainment until the early part of the twentieth century, when motion pictures replaced the last of these traveling shows (Simmons 1977:8).

Although less so today than during the years of isolation, the Hispanic villagers remain a self-reliant people. Whenever possible, they continue to provide for their own needs. Many families cut their own firewood rather than rely on commercial gas or electricity for heat. When the village church needs painting or replastering, the people do it themselves in a cooperative effort. The village way to make adobes for a new house is to buy a "kegger" and invite friends over, with the understanding that the beer will not be served until the adobes are finished. And getting a deer or elk on a hunting trip is still the time-honored symbol of a man's ability to provide for his family.

Procession, Contreras, New Mexico.

CHAPTER EIGHT

FEAST DAYS

The saints came to New Mexico with the first Spanish settlers. San Antonio, San Francisco, Santiago—they have always been an integral part of village life. Carried in the wagon trains of colonists and trade caravans, these examples of traditional European religious art arrived from Spain and Mexico during the first century of colonization to instruct and comfort the isolated people of the far northern frontier. By the late eighteenth century, the villages needed new holy statues and paintings to replace those lost through time and Indian warfare, and the role of the New Mexican santero evolved.

The Catholic saints symbolized the divine in human form and stood as paragons of devotion and wisdom, providing a link between earthly existence and heaven. In the homes of Hispanic villagers, they were often regarded as members of the family to be appropriately honored or scolded. It is still not uncommon to find a bulto with its face turned to the wall in retribution for an unanswered prayer.

The traditional cycle of Catholic feast days in Hispanic New Mexico, with roots in early Spain, was intended to pay homage to particular saints and religious happenings or to invoke heavenly blessings on certain community affairs. While ceremonies in Spain and New Mexico were similar, many local elaborations and interpretations have evolved over the centuries in response to village conditions and needs. The scarcity of priests and the lack of written records during the early years made it difficult for isolated villagers to fulfill the prescribed requirements of some Catholic ceremonies. Often, a celebration has been held year after year for its visual and emotional appeal, but with only partial understanding of its original purpose. Many traditional Spanish religious festivals have become folk festivals unique to the villages of Hispanic New Mexico.

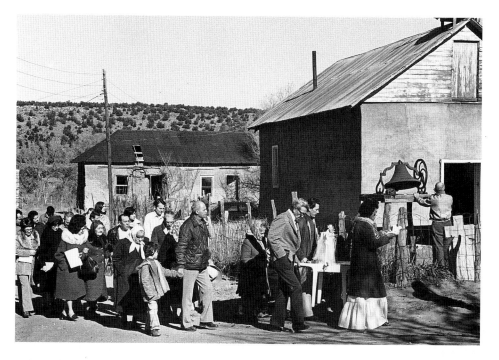

Procession in honor of the Immaculate Conception, El Cerrito, New Mexico.

Some rituals dating to the Spanish colonial period have probably not survived to the present day, and as meanings become obscure and relevance to contemporary village life is lost, many feasts decline in popularity and eventually are forgotten altogether. In 1942 it was noted that in the village of Arroyo Hondo, the once-popular ceremony known as *La Porciúncula* had almost completely disappeared within a short period of time. A watered-down version of the original ceremony was being attended by only a few older villagers (Rael 1942:83–86).

Since about 1975, other celebrations have also shown signs of becoming obsolete. Enthusiasm for the Corpus Christi procession has lessened in recent years, and the Easter tradition of blessing the food and the annual blessing of the cemetery are seldom observed. *El Día de Santa Ana*, often celebrated with a women's horse race, and the ancient *corrida de gallo*, an exciting contest of horsemanship and bravery in which the victim is a rooster, have not been seen for many years. The demise of the corrida, variously known as "the rooster race," "the rooster pull," or "playing the rooster," was brought about by several factors. In Tecolote, young men are learning to drive cars and trucks instead of the riding skills necessary for this difficult sport. In Villanueva, although young people still ride horses, the corrida tradition lapsed when their traditional arena, the main road of the village, was paved over. Recently, there has been talk of bringing back the custom in a nearby field or at the rodeo grounds.

In a few places, some of the old rituals have been revived in an attempt to recapture values from the past. After a five-year lapse, the town of Ojo Sarco recently celebrated the traditional *Pasear Los Santos*. A carved statue of Christ, resplendent in a gold-colored robe, was carried on a litter, while Santo Tomás, dressed in a brilliant red cloak, was held in the arms of the faithful during a five-mile procession along the dirt roads of their mountain valley. At intervals, the celebrants paused for the saints to see and bless the water in the ditches, the newly planted fields, and the grazing animals. At the halfway point, a mayordomo allowed the smoke from a dish of burning incense to envelope

Procession carrying the village santos, La Joya, New Mexico.

Procession, La Joya, New Mexico.

the santos. Afterwards, everyone retired to the mayordomo's home for a feast prepared by the women. The bultos surveyed the diners from a place of honor at the head of the table.

The feast day for San Isidro, patron saint of farmers, used to be observed in Córdova and Las Nutrias for many years to bless the fields and crops, and in some villages, the river was blessed on San Juan Day. In agrarian communities, great faith was placed in the intercession of the saints for a successful harvest, but agriculture has become less important in village life, and such rituals are seldom performed.

Although some fiestas are transitory or held in only a few towns, the feast day for the patron saint is common to all villages. This celebration has retained a popularity that transcends any question of its relevance to modern life and that continues to fulfill the religious and emotional needs of the people. At its founding, a Hispanic town is dedicated to a patron saint, whose hand-carved or plaster bulto is honored each year with *La Función del Santo*. This celebration, expressing the villagers' love of their saint, is often the most important religious and social event of the year.

Procession in honor of San Isidro, el Rancho de las Golondrinas, La Cienega, New Mexico.

Early accounts of patron-saint fiestas in New Mexico indicate that the religious rituals have remained essentially the same in most villages but that some traditional social activities have been dropped or replaced with forms of twentieth-century commercialism. The feast day in a small, remote village is more likely to have retained traditional elements than that in a town influenced by nearby urban areas. As an old Hispanic proverb observes, "Each saint has its day." Few weeks pass in which at least one of the Roman Catholic saints popular with the Hispanic people is not honored.

Preparations for the celebration begin far in advance under the direction of the village mayordomos. The church undergoes a thorough cleaning and redecoration. Fresh adobe plaster covers the outside walls, and the inside is repainted, often in shades of pink, yellow, or blue. Clean curtains appear at the windows, altar cloths are washed, and bright new flowers decorate the sanctuary and the litter that will carry the santo. In earlier days, flowers were often fashioned from scraps of colored paper or cloth, but today they are usually made of plastic. Every year the women create a new wardrobe for their bultos, sewing lovely long robes and cloaks and making new crowns and jewelry for them. Some churches have preserved their saint's clothes from the early part of the twentieth century—a record of evolving styles and materials.

The celebration begins on the evening before the feast day with vespers in the church. *Luminarias* (bonfires) light a path around the plaza. Some towns have a procession, or a dance in the schoolhouse. But the real festivities begin the following morning when the priest arrives in his splendid vestments and the church bell summons the people to worship. Families, neighbors, and friends welcome visitors and enter the church to join in the celebration of the Fiesta Mass and to receive Holy Communion. After the service, the image of the patron saint is taken from his place of honor before the altar and placed on a litter to be carried in procession by the mayordomos. In Bernal and Mora, as in many villages, a canopy, often decorated with flowers or streamers, is raised over the litter to shade the bulto from the sun. In Contreras and Las Nutrias, the saints are carried in the arms of the parishioners. The people and the priest follow the processional cross. In La Joya, colorful banners represent various church societies or carry religious messages. In Tierra Amarilla, the banners are carried by village men on horseback. Church bells, guitars, fiddles, and perhaps an accordian accompany the people as they offer prayers and sing hymns of praise to the saint. The procession slowly makes its way through the streets or around the plaza as the patron saint surveys and blesses the

Procession, Tecolote, New Mexico.

town. The bulto is then returned to its place in the church, the banners are stored, and the people leave for the secular activities of the feast day.

The patron saint's feast day is also an occasion to honor the outgoing mayordomos and turn over the office to new ones for the coming year. In Tecolote, on one feast day afternoon, the four retiring mayordomos relinquished their post in a church ceremony. Participants prayed the rosary and sang *"Despedida a la Virgin"* and *"Adios, O Madre"* to their patron saint, Our Lady of Sorrows—emotional songs of their love for her and their unhappiness at having to leave her. As the people sang, the old and new mayordomos circled around the bulto, which stood on a table before the altar. After the service, the parishioners pinned money on the outgoing mayordomos to thank them for their service during the past year.

An important part of village fiestas is *la cena* (the dinner), a sharing of food and friendship. In a small town like El Cerrito, the mayordomos invite everyone into their homes, where family and friends wait their turn to eat at long tables piled high with food. If a schoolhouse or other town building is available, such as the firehouse in Veguita, the

*Procession known as Pasear los Santos, Ojo Sarco,
New Mexico.*

women of the village usually prepare a community meal. In large towns like Chimayo, la cena is symbolized by food booths which sell hamburgers and soft drinks to raise money for the church and satisfy the hunger of the crowd.

A few villages have broadened secular elements of the patron-saint procession. Tierra Amarilla has humorous floats in its procession, and Chimayo now has two separate processions in its three-day celebration: one of a religious nature to carry the statue of Señor Santiago through the streets of the town, the other a parade which in recent years has featured a beauty queen, commercial floats, and a mariachi band.

Nonreligious activities have always been a part of most village feast days, and while some events such as gambling and the corrida de gallo have been discarded, others are as popular today as they were fifty years ago. La Joya and Chimayo hire local bands and singers, Veguita sets up a piñata for the children, and Villanueva sells rides on a horse-drawn wagon. Tecolote recently held a small carnival with homemade games and prizes of religious medals and stuffed animals. On many village plazas, everyone enjoys impromptu singing and guitar playing.

A few towns such as Mora have a rodeo as part of their feast days. Many of the participants are local cowboys demonstrating their skills before friends and neighbors, not rodeo professionals. The arena is usually a fenced-in field on the edge of town with an elevated judges' stand on one side and pens to hold the cattle. It is a casual affair where

Procession, Las Nutrias, New Mexico.

Procession in honor of Señor Santiago, Chimayo, New Mexico.

a lot of time is spent visiting with friends and where small boys learn the ropes by helping their fathers. The village rodeo is probably the most popular event of the fiesta.

The Hispanic love of folk drama and pageantry is apparent in the plays and dances performed during the village fiestas. In 1598 the first performance in New Mexico of *Los Moros y Cristianos* was held for the Indians of San Juan Pueblo by the newly arrived Spanish settlers. The story of the struggle and final triumph of Spanish Christianity over pagan Moorish forces continues to be popular. In Chimayo, it is performed on horseback as a part of the annual feast day by local actors wearing colorful costumes and carrying realistic swords and shields. During the show, twenty-four horsemen charge back and forth across the field between two imitation plywood castles in an exciting mock battle, shouting their lines in an old Spanish dialect while authentic Catalán music blares from a nearby loudspeaker. In the early Spanish versions of Los Moros y Cristianos, some of which date to the twelfth

Procession, Tierra Amarilla, New Mexico.

century, the plot was considerably more elaborate and often included sword dancing or singing (Foster 1960:221–25). The New Mexico version, performed entirely on horseback, appears to be a local innovation —possibly inspired by the figures of St. George or Santiago (St. James), who rode to the aid of Spanish Christians during battles with the

Breaking a piñata, Las Nutrias, New Mexico.

Moors. The old New Mexican santeros often depicted Santiago, dressed in early frontier clothing, riding over the slain bodies of the conquered Moors.

Bernalillo celebrates its feast day with a *Matachines* dance. The origin of this colorful dance-drama is unclear, but the costumes, music, and dance steps combine old- and new-world characteristics. The rainbows of ribbons cascading down the dancers' backs, the fringed headdresses decorated with beads and shiny Christmas ornaments, and the

Dancing at a feast day celebration, San Augustine, New Mexico.

Musicians at a feast day celebration, San Augustine, New Mexico.

Matachines dance, Bernalillo, New Mexico. This is a colorful dance-drama of Christian symbolism with comic overtones.

gourd rattle and three-pronged *palma* held in each hand represent Spanish, Moorish, and Aztec influences. A drama of Christian symbolism with comic overtones, the dance is acted out to the rhythmic melodies of fiddles and guitars (Champe 1983:4–5).

For almost four centuries, the Hispanic village fiestas have played an important role in village life, reflecting the religious devotion of the people and their joyous sense of celebration. They have survived in spite of changing mores and lifestyles because they continue to fill a need in the peoples' lives, linking them to the past and perpetuating important values into the future.

The struggle between Moors and Christians in medieval Spain reenacted in Chimayo, New Mexico.

REFERENCES

Baxter, Sylvester
1885 "Along the Rio Grande," *Harpers*, vol. 70, no. 419.

Bloom, John P.
1959 "New Mexico Viewed by Anglo-Americans, 1846–1849," *New Mexico Historical Review*, vol. 34, no. 3.

Bloom, Lansing R.
1936 "Bourke on the Southwest, X," *New Mexico Historical Review*, vol. 11, no. 3.

Brown, Lorin W.
1978 *Hispano Folklife of New Mexico* (Albuquerque: University of New Mexico Press).

Bunting, Bainbridge
1976 *Early Architecture of New Mexico* (Albuquerque: University of New Mexico Press).

Bunting, Bainbridge, Thomas R. Lyons, and Margil Lyons
1983 "Penitente Brotherhood Moradas and Their Architecture," in *Hispanic Arts and Ethnohistory in the Southwest*, edited by Marta Weigle, with Claudia L. Larcombe and Samuel Larcombe (Santa Fe: Ancient City Press).

Casarez, Maria Elena
1981 "The Tough Life of Sheep Ranchers in State," *New Mexican*, December 14.

Champe, Flavia Waters
1983 *The Matachines Dance of the Upper Rio Grande* (Lincoln: University of Nebraska Press).

Coles, Robert
1973 *The Old Ones of New Mexico* (Albuquerque: University of New Mexico Press).

Davis, W. W. H.
1857 *El Gringo or New Mexico and Her People* (New York: Harpers).

Dickey, Roland F.
1949 *New Mexico Village Arts* (Albuquerque: University of New Mexico Press).

Farrar, Harold R., ed.
1968 "Tales of New Mexico Territory—1868–1876," *New Mexico Historical Review*, vol. 43, no. 2.

Foster, George M.
1960 *Culture and Conquest: America's Spanish Heritage* (New York: Wenner-Gren Foundation for Anthropological Research).

Frazer, Robert W., ed.
1968 *New Mexico in 1850: A Military View* (Norman: University of Oklahoma Press).

Hackett, Charles Wilson, ed.
1937 *Historical Documents Relating to New Mexico, Nueva Vizcaya, and Approaches Thereto, to 1773.* Carnegie Institution, Publication no. 330, vol. 3 (Washington, D.C.).

Jenkins, Myra Ellen
1966 "Taos Pueblo and Its Neighbors," *New Mexico Historical Review*, vol. 41, no. 2.

Kenner, Charles L.
1969 *A History of New Mexican–Plains Indian Relations* (Norman: University of Oklahoma Press).

Kubler, George
1972 *The Religious Architecture of New Mexico* (Albuquerque: University of New Mexico Press).

La Iglesia de Santa Cruz de la Cañada
1983 La Iglesia de Santa Cruz de la Cañada: 1733–1983, 250th Anniversary (Santa Cruz, New Mexico).

Meinig, D. W.
1971 *Southwest: Three Peoples in Geographical Change, 1600–1970* (New York: Oxford University Press).

Mills, George, and Richard Grove
1956 *Lucifer and the Crucifer: The Enigma of the Penitentes* (Colorado Springs: Taylor Museum).

Milton, John R., ed.
1971 *Conversations with Frank Waters* (Chicago: Sage Books).

Pearce, T. M., ed.
1965 *New Mexico Place Names, a Geographical Dictionary* (Albuquerque: University of New Mexico Press).

Rael, Juan B.
1942 "New Mexican Spanish Feasts," *California Folklore Quarterly*, no. 1.

Ream, Glen O.
1980 *Out of New Mexico's Past* (Santa Fe: Sundial Books).

Samora, Julian, and Patricia Vandel Simon
1977 *A History of the Mexican-American People* (South Bend: University of Notre Dame Press).

Simmons, Marc
1977 "The Puppet Masters," *Santa Fe Reporter*, March 10.

Snow, David H.
1979   "Rural Hispanic Community Organization in Northern New Mexico: An Historical Perspective," in *The Colorado Studies: The Survival of Spanish American Villages*, no. 15, ed. by Paul Kutsche (Research Committee of Colorado College, Colorado Springs).

Townley, John M.
1971   "El Placer: A New Mexico Mining Boom Before 1846," *Journal of the West*, vol. 10, no. 1.

Van Ness, John R.
1979   "Hispanic Village Organization in Northern New Mexico: Corporate Community Structure in Historic and Comparative Perspective," in *The Colorado Studies: The Survival of Spanish American Villages*, no. 15, ed. by Paul Kutsche (Research Committee of Colorado College, Colorado Springs).

Wallrich, William
1951   "The Santero Tradition in the San Luis Valley, *Western Folklore*, vol. 10, no. 2.

Weber, David J., ed.
1967   *Albert Pike: Prose Sketches and Poems* (Albuquerque: Calvin Horn).

1973   *Foreigners in Their Native Land: Historical Roots of the Mexican Americans* (Albuquerque: University of New Mexico Press).

Weigle, Marta
1976   *Brothers of Light, Brothers of Blood: The Penitentes of the Southwest* (Albuquerque: University of New Mexico Press).

Wroth, William
1979   "The Flowering and Decline of the Art of the New Mexican Santero: 1780–1900," in *New Spain's Far Northern Frontier*, ed. by David J. Weber (Albuquerque: University of New Mexico Press).

1982   *Christian Images in Hispanic New Mexico* (Colorado Springs: Taylor Museum).